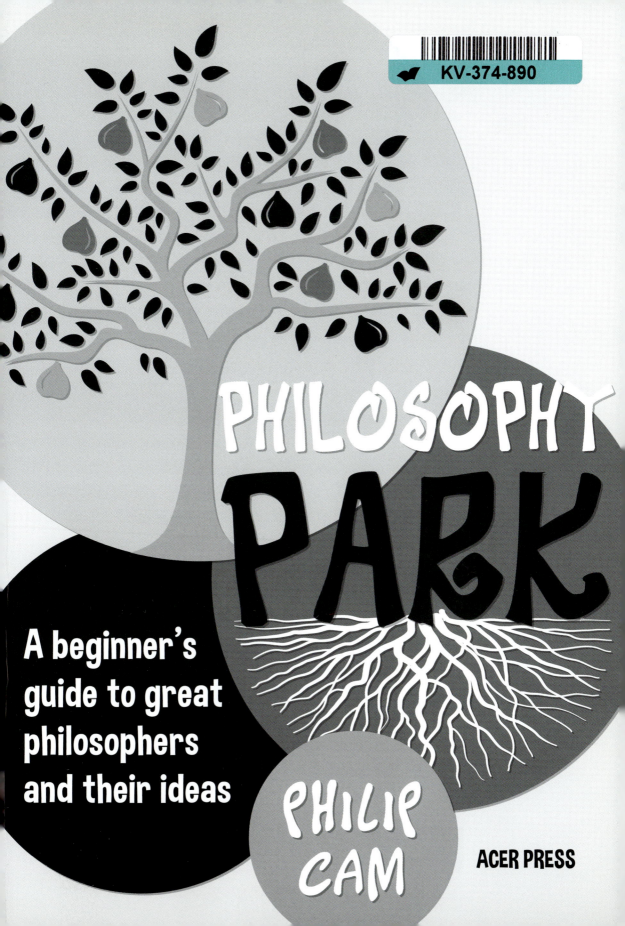

PHILOSOPHY PARK

A beginner's guide to great philosophers and their ideas

PHILIP CAM

ACER PRESS

First published 2013
by ACER Press, an imprint of
Australian Council *for* Educational Research Ltd
19 Prospect Hill Road, Camberwell, Victoria, 3124, Australia

www.acerpress.com.au
sales@acer.edu.au

Edited by Elisa Webb
Cover design, text design and typesetting by ACER Creative Services
Printed in Australia by Ego Print

National Library of Australia Cataloguing-in-Publication entry

Author: Cam, Philip, 1948- author.

Title: Philosophy park : a beginner's guide to great philosophers
and their ideas / Philip Cam.

ISBN: 9781742861913 (paperback)

Target Audience: For primary school age.

Subjects: Philosophers--Juvenile literature.
Philosophy--Juvenile literature.

Dewey Number: 180

PHILOSOPHY
PARK

CONTENTS

CONTENTS

THE IONIAN PHILOSOPHERS

THALES
c. 624–c. 546 BC

ANAXIMANDER
c. 610–c. 546 BC

ANAXIMENES
c. 585–c. 528 BC

Over two and a half thousand years ago, Greeks inhabited Ionia, the land along the coast of present-day Turkey. There, in the town of Miletus, lived three philosophers. The oldest was Thales, next was Anaximander, followed by the youngest, Anaximenes. Virtually nothing written by these philosophers has survived, and what little we know about them comes from what others wrote about them. They were so much discussed because they tried to understand the world through observation and reasoning rather than in terms of myths and legends, as those before them had done. In their thought we find the origins of science and philosophy.

These three philosophers were particularly interested in the origins of the world and from what it was made. Thales held that the world came from water, which produced all things, whether solid, liquid or gas. Anaximander reasoned that Thales was wrong in that not everything could come from water. For example, water puts out fire and the sun's heat dries up water, so water and fire are opposites, which tend to destroy one another. In fact, each of what the ancients thought of as the elements— air, earth, fire and water—were opposed to one another, so that the world could not have come from any one of them. It must have arisen from something else. Anaximander thought of this as an infinite or limitless substance. We are not sure exactly what he had in mind, but he must have thought that at some point the elements arose out of it. Finally, Anaximenes said that both Thales and Anaximander were wrong and that the world came from air or mist, which was squeezed together into water and squashed even further to make earth and rock, as well as being thinned out to make fire.

In the story that follows, you will find bats arguing about the beginning of the world. 'Earth, Air, Fire and Water' is based on the thought of Thales, Anaximander and Anaximenes.

Earth, Air, Fire and Water

THE PITCH BLACK OF night has swallowed everything up, as if returning us to the time before time began! As if there is nothing but the air we breathe, or we are adrift on an endless ocean where neither moon nor stars ever shine. Then out of the silence come twittering alien voices. There they are again. Bats! As our eyes slowly become accustomed to the dark, we can begin to see the outline of the giant fig tree in whose limbs they are hanging. Come closer and listen to what they are saying. The bats are discussing the beginning of the world.

'The world cannot have been made from nothing,' said Scratchy in his raspy little voice. 'If someone made the world, then they must have made it out of something.'

'If the world was made in the way that things can be made out of sticks and stones, then I agree with you,' squeaked Flappy. 'But what if no one made the world? What then?'

'Even if no one made the world,' Scratchy insisted, 'it must have been made from something.'

'Couldn't an event as mysterious as the beginning of the world have come about from nothing?' asked Flappy.

'No,' said Scratchy sharply. 'An event happens to *something*. It cannot happen to *nothing*.'

'I don't follow you, Scratchy. What do you mean?'

'I'll tell you what I mean,' Scratchy sighed. 'Take this tree. It has sprouted little figs that weren't here a month ago. Something has happened to make the figs grow. But it couldn't have happened without the tree. To get figs you must first have a fig tree.'

'Do you mean that to get worlds there must first be a *world tree*?' exclaimed Flappy excitedly.

'No, that's not what I mean,' said Scratchy dryly. 'Stop flapping about like a broken umbrella and think more carefully. I meant that first there was a fig tree without any figs and then something happened to the tree to make the figs grow. That's an event. And that's how it must have been with the beginning of the world. Something must have happened *to something* in order to create the world.'

'You may be right about ordinary events,' admitted Flappy. 'They do involve things changing. Yet it seems to me that if the world came about from nothing, that would also be an event.'

'It would be like no other event we know, Flappy.'

'But the beginning of the world *is* an event like no other we know, Scratchy.'

All the while, a bat named Big Black—or BB, for short—had been listening to this conversation. At first, he couldn't see the point of such silly chatter, and so he continued munching on the figs that had sprouted on the giant fig tree that stood at the centre of the park. BB reckoned that Flappy and Scratchy hadn't a clue as to what made the tree produce those delicious little figs right under their noses. So how could they figure out something as grand and distant as the beginning of the world? Yet, as BB ate he got to thinking and now he had an idea. Not that he was going to blurt it out straightaway. BB began by preparing the ground.

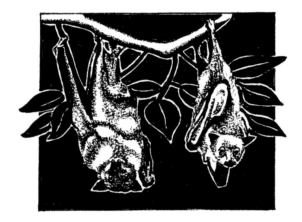

'Hey, Scratchy, if everything in this world originally came from something, what do you suppose it was?'

'Well, BB, I believe that once there was only water and everything came from that.'

'Water ... hmm. Why water?'

'Just think about it. Watery stuff comes out of all sorts of things. Trees have sap, figs are juicy and it rains from the sky. Even the grass gives off steam as it heats in the sun on a winter's morning.'

'Like fresh dog poo,' Flappy tittered. 'That gives off steam too.'

'Just like you to think of that,' Scratchy shot back, and then continued talking to BB. 'Don't forget that we are also made up almost entirely of water. Of all the elements—earth, air, fire and water—it seems that water is common to everything. Therefore, it is the thing of which they might all be made.'

'You've got water on the brain,' cried Flappy, who had been listening to Scratchy with growing disbelief. 'You might as well say that everything is made of air.'

'Why air?' asked BB.

'Water is drawn up into the air to make clouds, as well as coming out of the air as rain,' replied Flappy. 'Fire cannot exist without air in order to burn, just as we can't exist without air in order to breathe. Even trees need air. They take in the air that we breathe out.'

'Yes, just like we breathe in the air that dogs fart out,' scoffed Scratchy.

'You can make fun of me if you like,' replied Flappy, 'but my reasons for saying that everything is made of air are just as good as your reasons for saying that everything is made of water.'

'And you think that your idea is better,' added Scratchy.

'No,' replied Flappy. 'I didn't say that.'

This was the moment for which BB had been waiting. '*I have a better idea*,' he said in a quiet, confident tone.

'You do?' the others exclaimed.

'Yes, *I do*,' replied BB, and went on swinging gently on his branch.

'Well, tell us,' demanded Flappy.

'Yes, do tell us, p-l-e-a-s-e,' echoed Scratchy.

'Very well, then,' replied BB, now that they were all ears. 'It is the Infinite.'

'The Infinite!' repeated Scratchy.

'The *what*?' said Flappy, who had never heard of such a thing.

'The Infinite,' repeated BB calmly. 'Unlike everything else in this world, the Infinite exists always and everywhere. It is not like water, which is found in one place but not another. Or like air, which comes and goes like the wind. The Infinite is boundless and everlasting.'

'Wow!' exclaimed Scratchy in amazement, with a shake of his leathery wings.

'And how do you suppose this thing of yours brought about the world?' asked Flappy, who was not prepared to be swept away by something he didn't understand.

'I have no idea,' replied BB. 'You admitted yourself that the beginning of the world was an awfully mysterious event. But there is one thing I do know. If there was something before the world, it must have existed forever.'

'And why is that?' asked Flappy.

'It is because otherwise you can always go on to ask where that thing came from.'

'I don't get it, BB,' Scratchy sighed, beginning to feel lost.

'Look at it like this, Scratchy,' BB said gently. 'You might as well say that first of all there was a stone, and the whole world came from that. But where did the stone come from?' Scratchy scratched his head and stared into the night with his big black eyes. 'From another stone?' he suggested hopefully.

'Ah! But then you will need another stone, and yet another, and so on *forever*,' BB replied. 'No, Scratchy, the only way out is to say that whatever the world sprang from was always there.'

'Unless the world came from nothing,' Flappy interjected.

'What on earth do you mean?' exclaimed BB.

'I mean just what I said,' Flappy insisted. 'For all we know, there was no time or space before the world came about. There was nothing at all—and no such thing as the Infinite.'

'I grant you that there was nothing our feeble bat brains can understand,' replied BB coolly. 'But who can claim to understand the Infinite?'

'The Infinite is just something you made up to explain how the world came about,' complained Flappy.

'That may be so, Flappy, but at least I don't face the embarrassment of suggesting that the world began from nothing at all.'

Flappy slowly opened and closed his wings as he mulled over BB's remark. 'You say that the Infinite is something our feeble bat brains cannot understand,' he said at last. 'In that case, none of us can possibly understand what you're talking about.'

The bats were stunned by Flappy's observation and hung motionless from their branches like washing on the line. If their poor bat brains couldn't possibly understand the Infinite, then BB could not possibly know what he meant by it. That such a deep-sounding idea might really be meaningless had dumbfounded them.

So the discussion between the bats came to an end. And suddenly the park that was as black as a world without eyes was as silent as a world without ears.

SOCRATES

c. 469–399 BC

Before Socrates, ancient Greek philosophy was concerned with the natural world, as we saw with the Ionian philosophers. Socrates turned attention away from nature to think about life and society. He was interested in how we should live, and thought that philosophy could tell us how to do so. In fact, he is supposed to have said that the unexamined life is not worth living, and that the pursuit of philosophy is the best way to live. He was noted for holding philosophical discussions in the streets of Athens with all kinds of people, young and old alike.

Rather than suggesting that he had all the answers, Socrates claimed to be ignorant. Not more ignorant than others, mind you, for he found that those who claimed to be wise were ignorant as well. In fact, he was wiser than they were, in knowing that he was ignorant when they did not.

It seems that Socrates wrote nothing. The best account we have of how he went about his discussions comes from the philosopher Plato, one of his students, who wrote dialogues in which Socrates is the main character. 'The Dawn Chorus' is based on Plato's characterisation of Socrates and you will have no difficulty recognising him in the story. He was not a handsome man and he had a snub nose.

The fate of Socrates was tragic. He was accused of introducing false gods into Athens and of corrupting the young through his teaching. Socrates was found guilty of the charges and condemned to death. Although he could have pleaded for a lesser penalty such as banishment, or arranged to escape from custody, he was not prepared to do so. And so he was executed by being made to drink hemlock.

THE DAWN CHORUS

THE BATS HAVE LONG gone when the first light of day begins to filter through the trees of a hushed and expectant park. Now the birds take their turn. First one bird and then another heralds the arrival of the sun. There are long low notes and short shrill ones, harsh and melodious tones. We hear every call imaginable, from squeaks and screeches, warbles and whistles, to cries and cackles, tweets and trills.

In the hollow of an old gum tree, Snub Nose is laughing out loud. He is forever laughing at one thing or another. He seems to see the funny side of life. No one can remember why he is called Snub Nose. It must be a joke, because he has such a long and powerful beak.

Snub Nose is calling the young birds to him, as he does every day. Snub Nose is their teacher. At least, he is like a teacher, except that he says he has nothing to teach. The young birds flock to him all the same. Something must attract them. We see that a magpie is already talking to Snub Nose.

'Do you think that bat philosophy is a good philosophy, Snub Nose—so that I should devote myself to finding out what the world is made of and from where it came?'

'Unfortunately, Maggie, I don't know how to answer your question.'

'Really, Snub Nose? How can that be? You know about the philosophy of the bats, as well as many other ways of looking at the world.'

'That is true, but it doesn't help. My problem is that I don't know what makes something good. And without first knowing what makes a thing good, I can't advise you as to whether the philosophy of the bats is a good philosophy. Do you see what I mean, Maggie?'

'I'm not sure, Snub Nose. Would you explain it to me again?'

'Let me put it like this. In order to know that what you are choosing is good, you first have to know what it is for something to be good. Isn't that so?'

'That is so, Snub Nose.'

'And if you think that you know what makes things good when really you do not, then you may think that something is good, when really it is not. Do you agree?'

'Yes, Snub Nose. You could end up choosing what you think is good, when in fact it is not.'

'My thought exactly, Maggie.'

'But surely, Snub Nose, knowing what it is for something to be good is not so difficult.'

'Perhaps it is easier to know such things when you are young and your mind is fresh, Maggie. So why don't you say what you think it is?'

'If you think that might help, Snub Nose.'

'It could hardly be a hindrance to say what you think, Maggie.'

'I was thinking that my mother brought me a worm first thing this morning, and it was a very good worm.'

'Ah, Maggie, we are off to a flying start. Straightaway you have come up with an example of something good. Well done! Now, can you say what made it good?'

'That's easy, Snub Nose. It was fat and juicy.'

'So being fat and juicy makes something good, you say.'

'It makes a worm good to eat.'

'And is being fat and juicy what makes other things good as well?'

'Not always. A good worm is fat and juicy, and so is a good fig. But a good seed is not fat and juicy. It is crisp and crunchy.'

'And a good beak—is it fat and juicy?'

'A good beak isn't fat and juicy, Snub Nose. What a silly thing to say. You should know what makes a good beak, because you have one yourself. A good beak is strong and powerful.'

'So it seems that being fat and juicy isn't the same thing as being good, Maggie. It is true of some good things, but not of others.'

'Yes, Snub Nose, not everything good is fat and juicy.'

'And not everything fat and juicy is good.'

'Isn't that saying the same thing?'

'No, Maggie. Even if everything good were fat and juicy, it wouldn't follow that everything fat and juicy must be good. There could still be fat and juicy things that aren't good.'

'Do you mean like caterpillars, Snub Nose? They are fat and juicy, but some of them are not good to eat because they are poisonous.'

'How true, Maggie! How true! You are doing so well today that I wonder whether you can say what we have discovered so far.'

'I'll try, Snub Nose, but then you must say whether you think I have got it right. For "fat and juicy" to be the same as "good" all good things must be fat and juicy *and* all fat and juicy things must be good.'

'I couldn't have put it better myself, Maggie! You're such a clever bird. Now here's a really hard question—but one we must be able to answer in order to say what makes something good: what do worms, figs, seeds and beaks all have in common that makes them good?'

'That they don't share with poisonous caterpillars?'

'Yes, we need something that they have in common with each other, but which they don't share with other things that aren't good.'

'I have no idea, Snub Nose. What's the answer?'

'Don't expect that I have the answer, Maggie. Remember, I said that I don't know what it is for something to be good.'

'I guess that I understand your problem now, Snub Nose. I thought that I knew what makes things good, but now I can see that I don't really know, either. It's funny. I know what makes a worm good to eat, or some caterpillars not good to eat, but not what "good" means in general.'

'Don't despair, Maggie. You have made great progress. You have discovered that you don't know what you thought you knew.'

'To know that you don't know isn't to know very much, Snub Nose.'

'Ah-ha-ha-ha-ha! To know that you don't know is no small thing, Maggie. There are those who spend their entire lives thinking that they know things they don't really know. And they either get angry or bury their heads in the sand if it is ever suggested that they don't really know what they think they know.'

'Knowing that I don't really know what I thought I knew only makes me want to know all the more, Snub Nose. It really starts me thinking.'

'Good for you, Maggie! Good for you! And with luck you will get some help. Here comes Rainbow. Let's ask him what it means for something to be good.'

While Rainbow wasn't much older than Maggie, he acted like a grown-up. He ate whatever he liked, screeched whenever he felt like it and went about town all by himself. Rainbow was a clever bird who quickly understood what Maggie and Snub Nose had been talking about. In no time at all he surprised them with a suggestion.

'As I understand it, you are looking for something that is common to all things said to be good. Well then, what about *pleasure?*'

'What about pleasure?' Snub Nose replied.

'All things said to be good are pleasurable,' responded Rainbow.

'All things or only some?' queried Snub Nose.

'Eating a fat and juicy worm is pleasurable,' replied Rainbow, 'and so is eating a nice juicy fig or a crisp and crunchy seed.'

'And having a *good beak*?' Snub Nose persisted. 'What about that?'

'It's such a pleasure to have a good beak that you can use for all manner of things and that is the envy of everyone,' replied Rainbow.

'Hmm ... ' mused Snub Nose, and began staring into space as if lost in thought.

'What about the caterpillar?' Maggie interjected.

'Ah, yes, the caterpillar,' squawked Rainbow. 'A poisonous caterpillar is not good because it gives you a tummy ache. That's the opposite of pleasure.'

'Snub Nose,' called Maggie, 'is it right that all good things are pleasurable?'

'Right?' said Snub Nose.

'Yes, could Rainbow be right?'

'I am not sure whether all good things are pleasurable,' admitted Snub Nose. 'But Rainbow has made a good suggestion when the two of us were stumped. I have been wondering, however, what happens if we look at it the other way around, and ask whether it is true that all things pleasurable are good. Don't forget that if the good and the pleasurable are really one and the same thing, then all things pleasurable must be good as well as all good things being pleasurable.'

'You mean like eating figs all day can be pleasurable, but it isn't good for you?' suggested Maggie.

'Maggie, you're a wonder! That's exactly the kind of thing I mean,' said Snub Nose.

'Wait a minute,' interjected Rainbow, 'if you keep on eating figs all day long then you'll feel sick.'

'That's my point, Rainbow,' replied Maggie. 'It shows that not everything pleasurable is good.'

'But eating too many figs isn't pleasurable,' squawked Rainbow. 'It's sickening.'

'Even though you don't feel good after eating too many figs, they still *taste* good,' said Maggie.

'Not to me,' replied Rainbow. 'When I have eaten too many figs, the very thought of pecking on a fig brings a sickening taste to my mouth.'

'Please help us, Snub Nose,' pleaded Maggie. 'Tell us who is right, Rainbow or me. Is everything pleasurable good or not?'

'Ah-ha-ha-ha, Maggie,' replied Snub Nose. 'Even if Rainbow is right about figs, it doesn't follow that everything pleasurable is good.'

'So we still don't really know for sure what the good is,' said Maggie.

'Dear me, no,' chuckled Snub Nose. 'But you and Rainbow have made progress in finding out. Besides, you have learned that everything good must share something in common that makes it good. Don't forget that.'

'Yes, Snub Nose. And it is something that other things lack,' added Maggie.

'Quite so,' said Snub Nose.

'Are you sure about all that, Snub Nose?' asked Rainbow.

'Sure about what, Rainbow?'

'Are you sure that all good things must have something in common that makes them good, and that other things lack?'

'Yes. Why do you ask?'

'Well,' said Rainbow, 'there might be nothing that all good things have in common which makes them good. Worms are good to eat when they are fat and juicy, while seeds are good when they are crisp and crunchy, just as beaks are good when they are strong and powerful. Different things could be good in different ways.'

'Just suppose for a moment that you were right, Rainbow,' replied Snub Nose. 'Then we wouldn't know what it means to ask what makes a worm, a seed, or a beak *good*. In order to ask such things, we must first have the idea of things being good, mustn't we? There must be something that allows us to apply the same word to all those different things.'

'I suppose so,' said Rainbow.

'Don't suppose it is so just because I say so, Rainbow,' Snub Nose chortled. 'There is very little that I can claim to know for certain. The best I can do is to teach young birds like you and Maggie to think for yourselves. Now if the two of you will excuse me, I still haven't had breakfast. And I have spotted a fat and juicy worm—a very *good* worm, if I may say so.'

With that remark, Snub Nose flew off across the park, laughing all the way.

PLATO

c. 429–347 BC

Plato lived in Athens and started a school of philosophy called the Academy. Along with his pupil Aristotle, Plato is the most influential thinker in the history of Western philosophy. He is also the earliest Greek philosopher whose writings have come down to us. They are composed of dialogues in which people think together about philosophical questions and problems—much as the characters do in this book.

Socrates is the main character in Plato's dialogues, which often makes it difficult to tell whether Plato is presenting his own views or those of his teacher. While Plato builds upon the thought of Socrates, he definitely comes into his own when he introduces what is known as his theory of ideas. Plato held that nothing in our everyday world is perfect. Nothing is perfectly good, beautiful or just, for example. Perfect goodness, beauty and justice exist only as ideas. Plato thought of these ideas as eternal and as more real than the things that we see about us. He held that everyday things were imperfect copies of those in an ideal world.

Plato explained how this relates to our everyday experience in his Parable of the Cave. He imagined prisoners who have been chained up their entire lives to face the wall of a cave, upon which a fire at the back of the cave projects the shadows of things passing behind the prisoners. They never get to see the things themselves, and mistake the shadows for reality. While this was like the way that he took most people to live, Plato thought of the philosopher as someone who was freed from the chains and came to know the difference between appearance and reality. Watch out for a version of Plato's cave in 'Scruffy, Mutt and the Ideal Dog'.

SCRUFFY, MUTT AND THE IDEAL DOG

SCRUFFY AND MUTT ARE the greatest of friends. They often disagree with each other, but they never fight. They know the difference between disagreeing with what someone says and snarling and snapping at them. The two stray dogs like to stroll around the park while the day is young and no one is about, and as they walk they love to talk about their lives and the world in which they live.

'Did I ever tell you that I come from a family of show dogs, Mutt?'

'I can't imagine you as a show dog, Scruffy. You don't look the type.'

'No, Mutt, and I never was. Even when I was little my fur was always tangled and I looked a mess, no matter how much I was brushed.'

'No wonder they called you Scruffy.'

'I was such a scruffy puppy that the breeder was willing to give me to anyone who would take me, but no one wanted me and in the end I decided to run away and make a life for myself on the streets.'

'At least you have fur,' Mutt grumbled. 'Just look at me. It's a wonder that they didn't call me Baldy.'

'None of us is perfect,' Scruffy volunteered. 'Even the best show dogs have imperfections. Their colour is too dark, their muzzle is too short, their coat is too long, or something is not quite right.'

'They're perfect by comparison with us,' said Mutt.

'But not by comparison with the ideal dog,' replied Scruffy.

'Didn't you just claim that none of us is perfect, Scruffy? In which case, there is no such thing as the ideal dog.'

'Oh, there is such a thing as the ideal dog, Mutt. Only it isn't one of us.'

'What do you mean?' said Mutt. 'Sometimes I can't make head or tail of what you say.'

'Then I will explain it to you,' replied Scruffy. 'Take judges at dog shows. They don't just compare one dog with another. They compare them all to the ideal dog—or rather to the ideal poodle, the ideal corgi, or the ideal Dalmatian. How could they measure the dogs of this world against the ideal if there were no ideal dog with which to compare them?'

'What you say is kind of right, Scruffy. Except that the ideal poodle or the ideal Dalmatian is only the dog lover's *idea* of the perfect poodle or Dalmatian. It doesn't actually exist. It isn't something real.'

'Come on, Mutt! Next you will be telling me that there is no such thing as a real circle.'

'Why would I be telling you that?'

'Because none of those things that we regard as circles—like roundabouts or bicycle wheels—are perfectly circular.'

'I agree that such things aren't perfectly circular, Scruffy, although some of them are more perfect than others.'

'You are right about that, Mutt. Yet we couldn't judge how good any of them are if there were no such thing as a perfect circle with which to compare them.'

'I see,' said Mutt. 'So you're saying that there must be such a thing as an ideal or perfect circle in order for us to be able to judge that something like a wheel or a roundabout isn't perfectly circular.'

'That's right, Mutt. That's exactly what I mean.'

'And are you also saying that there must be a perfect poodle and a perfect Dalmatian, against which we can judge the imperfections of ordinary poodles and Dalmatians?'

'Something like that,' said Scruffy.

'But no one has ever seen a perfect circle or an ideal dog, Scruffy. How can we judge actual dogs and circles by comparing them with things that we have never seen?'

'We see them with our mind's eye, Mutt.'

'We see them with our mind's eye? What on earth does that mean?'

'But that's just it! The perfect circle and the ideal dog aren't on earth. They are things that we perceive in our minds rather than through our senses.'

'Wouldn't that make the perfect circle and the ideal dog weird kinds of things? If we can see them only with our minds, then they must be very different from the circles and dogs that we see with our eyes.'

'That's what I meant when I said that the ideal dog isn't one of us, Mutt. The ideal dog is something that no breeder can produce, just as the perfect circle is something that no one can make, no matter how hard they try. They are not in the world that we see with our eyes, but in the world that we perceive with our minds.'

By this time Mutt and Scruffy had reached the pond where they always stopped to drink. As Mutt watched Scruffy lapping at the water he became fascinated by the way it made ripples that wrinkled their reflections.

'Say, Scruffy,' he began, 'I can see a couple of dogs that are even scruffier than us.'

'Where?' barked Scruffy.

'Just look in the water and you will see them. See how wrinkly and rippled they are.'

'Mutt, sometimes you amaze me.'

'I know that they aren't *real* dogs, Scruffy. I'm not that silly. They are just our reflections in the water.'

'No, I meant that your observation is a stroke of genius.'

'Whatever do you mean, Scruffy?'

'Well, you have just said that the dogs in the water are only our wrinkled reflections.'

'Yes. What of it?'

'Don't you see, Mutt? That's how we compare to the ideal dog.'

'No, Scruffy, I don't see.'

'What I am saying is that just as the dogs in the water are only our rippled reflections, so we are only poor reflections of the ideal dog.'

'Come off it, Scruffy! How can you compare us to our reflections? We are real dogs and our reflections are not.'

'We may be real dogs, Mutt, but we are not as real as the ideal dog.'

'How do you figure that out?'

'Because the ideal dog is everything a dog should be and ever more will be so, while we are but poor reflections of such a dog and our lives are as fleeting as the play of light upon the water.'

'That sounds very deep, Scruffy. Yet it seems to me that, if we accepted your comparison, it would turn out that all the things we see about us aren't *really* real. Only things like the ideal dog and the perfect circle are real.'

'That's right, Mutt. I might just as well have pointed to those dogs that spend their lives stretched out upon the sofa with their eyes glued to the television. Do you know the kind of dog I mean?'

'I do, Scruffy. I have also heard of children who spend most of their waking hours glued to screens like that.'

'Right, Mutt. Now imagine a pack of dogs that were brought up in a darkened room and chained up so that their eyes were always fixed upon the television.'

'So that they never saw anything but what was on television?'

'That's exactly what I mean. The dogs would mistake the images on the television for the real thing, wouldn't they?'

'I suppose they would, Scruffy.'

'Now suppose that one of the dogs was taken from the room and shown the outside world, so that he saw the actual things that were only pictured on television.'

'Hot dog! I think that at first he might be very confused. Yet after a while he would discover that what he had taken to be the real world was only the world as it appears on television, and that the images that appeared on the screen were not the things themselves. I'll bet he would be amazed at his discovery.'

'No doubt he would be astounded to find out the truth, Mutt. Now let us suppose that he was taken back to the darkened room so that he could tell the other dogs what he had discovered. How do you think they would respond?'

'They would probably think that he was mad, Scruffy. They might even turn on him if he kept whining on about all of them being deluded into thinking that the pictures on the screen were the things themselves.'

'It is as you say, Mutt! And aren't we like the dogs chained up in the darkened room? We think the images that light casts upon our eyes show us the world as it is in reality. So if someone were to say that we see nothing but appearances, and that the world in reality is something quite different, they would be thought to be as mad as that dog.'

'No doubt you are right about that, Scruffy. Yet what about such things as the perfect circle and the ideal dog, which you say we can perceive with our mind's eye? Are they also mere appearances?'

'No, Mutt, they are like the world that the chained-up dogs never see—the reality that lies behind the appearances.'

'So what are *really* real are those things that we can perceive with our minds and not the impressions that come to our senses.'

'That's what I have been suggesting all along, Mutt.'

'So the ideal dog and the perfect circle that we inwardly perceive are real, while what we take to be dogs and circles in the world about us are mere appearance?'

'That would be so, Mutt. What do you think?'

'I'm not sure what to think, Scruffy. Except, couldn't it be the other way around?'

'What do you mean, the other way around?'

'I mean that the things we perceive in the world about us are real, while those that appear before our inner eye are merely ideas conjured up in our minds.'

'Why do you always have to tip everything over and turn it upside down, Mutt?'

'I'm sorry, Scruffy. I didn't mean to upset you. I just thought that maybe there is no such thing as a perfect circle— not *really*—while there are such things as bicycle wheels and roundabouts.'

'You might say that, Mutt. But there wouldn't be any bicycle wheels or roundabouts if the ideas of them had never suggested themselves to anyone; and how could those ideas have come to mind if no-one ever had the idea of a circle in the first place?'

'So you're saying that first there must be the idea of a circle and the idea of a bicycle wheel or a roundabout for bicycle wheels or roundabouts to be invented.'

'Not only that. We couldn't see bicycle wheels and roundabouts as circular if we didn't have the idea of a circle in our minds in the first place.'

'So we see things with our minds rather than just with our eyes, Scruffy? Is that what you mean?'

'You are a genius, Mutt! What would I do without you? Without ideas, we couldn't make sense of anything we saw. We would have no *idea* of what we were looking at.'

'I have a very clear idea of what I am looking at, Scruffy.'

'I am sure that you do, Mutt. What is it?'

'It is the dog catcher coming down the path.'

Scruffy glanced over his shoulder and then looked back at Mutt. The two of them must have had the same idea, because they both scampered away in the other direction.

ARISTOTLE

384–322 BC

Aristotle was Plato's pupil. Like the Ionian philosophers, he was intensely curious about the natural world, but he also thought a great deal about how we should live. Among other things, he wrote about science, reasoning, politics, ethics and the arts. In fact, he wrote on so many things that his work became the first comprehensive system of philosophy. Aristotle made mighty contributions to the knowledge of his day, and was regarded as a great authority in many fields for two thousand years. Like Plato, he began a school in Athens, which was called the Lyceum.

'The Golden Mean' takes us into Aristotle's ethics. Like most of us, Aristotle thought that the greatest good for a person is to be happy and live well. Yet what is happiness? Of what does it consist? Aristotle said that in order to answer this question we need to consider what makes us distinctively human. After all, happiness for a human being is not the same as happiness for a cow. He claimed that we differ from other creatures because we have the power of reason, and that it is only through the proper exercise of our reason that we can have a happy life. It is only by exercising good judgment and behaving in a reasonable fashion that we can cultivate virtues such as generosity, patience and courage. That is what we need in order to live well.

Aristotle conceived each of the virtues as a Golden Mean that lies between two vices. Courage stands between cowardice and foolhardiness, for example, with the coward lacking courage and the foolhardy being reckless. Similarly, it is stingy to be ungenerous, while it is extravagant to go too far in the other direction. In each case, we need to exercise good judgment in the circumstances in order to make the right decision. Virtue lies in intelligently seeking moderation in all things, which Aristotle saw as the road to happiness.

THE GOLDEN MEAN

EVERY DAY, AFTER BREAKFAST, Bob comes to read the morning paper on the bench under the tree that stands at the centre of the park. His friend Larry often joins him, and the two elderly men sit and talk, enjoying each other's company. Today something in the paper seems to have particularly caught Bob's attention, because as Larry approaches he can hear his friend chuckling to himself behind the outstretched news.

'What's up, Bob?'

'Ah, Larry, listen to this. A couple has won the lottery and instantly become wealthy beyond their wildest dreams.'

'Half their luck! I wish my fairy godmother would sprinkle some lucky stardust over me. I'll bet they are happy as happy can be.'

'You could say that they are as happy as Larry.'

'I might have known you couldn't resist that wisecrack, Bob.'

'Actually, it says here that they are the happiest people in the world.'

'That's the same as saying that they are over the moon about their win. You're not meant to take it literally. No doubt they are extremely happy.'

'They are happy now, Larry, but will it last? Will they still be happy as the years go by, just because they came into a fortune?'

'I know they say that money can't buy happiness, Bob, but winning the lottery can set you up for life.'

'Maybe it's easier to be happy if you are well-off, Larry, but being wealthy is not the same as being happy.' Bob removed his glasses and began cleaning them. 'Wealth is like health,' he said after a while. 'It is easier to be happy if you have good health, but being healthy isn't the same as being happy. There are plenty of healthy people who aren't happy, just as some people are miserable even though they're rich.'

'True enough, Bob. Yet if being wealthy and healthy cannot guarantee happiness, then what can?'

'Maybe there is no guarantee that you'll have a happy life, Larry. If only working out how to be happy were like working out a sum in arithmetic, where you can be sure to get the right answer so long as you don't make mistakes.'

'You can go wrong in working out how to live your life, just as you can in arithmetic.'

'You're right about that, Larry. Anyone who figures that they'll be made happy by just making money has made that mistake.'

'So what would you say makes for happiness in life, Bob? You've had a happy life, so you must have some idea.'

Bob didn't answer Larry immediately but went on cleaning his glasses. 'I would say,' he said at last, 'that a happy life is a fulfilled one.'

'That sounds right, Bob, but it only leads to another question. What is a fulfilled life?'

'It's one that makes the most of your potential.'

'It's all very well to say that fulfilment is the realisation of your potential, Bob, but we seem to be going around in circles.'

'Then let me try again and see if I can explain myself more fully. What do you think it would be for a cow to be happy?'

'I guess that a cow would be happy to spend its life grazing in the fields.'

'So far as we know, that's right, Larry. That is fulfilment for a cow. Yet if *we* were to spend *our* lives just wandering around eating like cows, that would hardly be fulfilling for us. We wouldn't be making the most of our potential, would we?'

'No, we would not.'

'So what makes us different from cows, Larry? And don't say it's because we have only two legs!'

'I understand perfectly well what you mean, Bob. You know I wouldn't say something silly like that.'

'OK, Larry. Calm down and tell me what you suppose the difference to be.'

'I would say that we can think and reason about the world in ways that cows cannot.'

'That's what I would say too, Larry. We have a great potential to think and therefore to do all kinds of things that cows can't do.'

'Doesn't that raise a problem, Bob? Since people can think, they have the power to do all kinds of things that aren't fulfilling—bad things that lead to misery rather than happiness.'

'That's a good point, Larry. In order to be happy we obviously need to use our reason in the right kind of way.'

'And what is the right kind of way?'

Bob slowly twirled his glasses around. Then he popped them back on his head. 'The right way to do things, Larry, is to behave as a virtuous person would.'

'That may be so, Bob, but it doesn't help very much unless we understand what it is to be virtuous.'

'That's true, Larry. If the happy person is one who uses their reason to behave as a virtuous person would, then we need to know what it is to be virtuous if we are to understand happiness.'

'Well then, Bob, what is it to be virtuous? You tell me that.'

'My goodness, you're a hard taskmaster, Larry. There I was, reading the morning paper, when you come along and ask me one question after another. If you keep on like that I am going to end up quite exhausted.'

'Sorry, Bob. I was getting carried away because the topic is so interesting. I'll tell you what. Why don't I try to answer my own question while you go on reading? If I come up with something, I'll stop you and we can continue our conversation.'

Bob smiled at Larry over the top of his glasses. Nothing more was needed to signal agreement between them. Then Bob unfurled his newspaper and continued reading, leaving Larry to his own thoughts.

While Bob was buried in his newspaper, Larry thought on and off about virtue, but mostly he just watched the passers-by. He nodded at a woman in a smart suit who hurried by carrying a bag stuffed with papers and shouting into her phone. He watched a workman from the council sitting on a wall and looking at the leaves he was there to rake. Suddenly Larry had an idea.

'Bob!'

'What's up?'

'You know how some people are always working and can never relax even for a moment, while other people don't do a stitch of work and can hardly bother to get out of their own way?'

'Yes. What of it?'

'In my experience, people who work themselves into the ground are seldom happy. They have no time to enjoy themselves. Yet lazy people aren't happy either. They accomplish very little and often feel depressed.'

'No doubt you're right, Larry. What's your point?'

'Well, there is a happy medium, isn't there? It's good to work and accomplish things, but not good to work so much that you never have a moment to relax.'

'Do you mean that it is good to have balance in your life?'

'It's either that or to keep things in proportion. In any case, I was thinking that someone who doesn't go to either extreme is likely to be happier than someone who does.'

'That's an interesting thought, Larry. Do you think it applies to other things besides work?'

'What do you mean?'

'Well, the couple I was reading about in the paper are wondering about what they are going to do with all the money they won in the lottery. They could go completely overboard and spend it on each and every whim, or they could salt it away and not spend a cent. But they are likely to be happier if they spend their money in moderation.'

'Yes, and they might be generous and give some of the money to charities, rather than refusing to offer any or giving it all away.'

'So your idea of getting the right proportion in things doesn't apply just to being diligent, Larry, but seems to also relate to other things like being sensible with money. Do you know what? I think that we might be onto something. Being diligent, rather than being a lazy good-for-nothing or a complete workaholic, is a virtue in a person, and so is being prudent with money rather than being either a spendthrift or a miser.'

'That's good, Bob. Can you think of other examples of getting the balance right?'

'Rather than that, let's do it the other way around. Why don't you give me something that you would say is a virtue in someone?'

'OK. What about being brave? That's a good quality in a person.'

'I agree. Is being brave also a matter of getting the right balance between two things, neither of which is agreeable?'

'That's a tough question, Bob.'

'Then let's break it down, and start on one side. What is it not to be anywhere near as brave as one should be?'

'It is to lack courage or to be a coward, Bob.'

'I agree. Now, on the other side, would it be brave to leap into danger, no matter what?'

'No, Bob. That would be reckless or foolhardy.'

'So the brave person neither runs away in a cowardly fashion nor rashly rushes into danger, but faces it in a reasonable way, understanding the risks involved. Isn't that so?'

'That's right, Bob. Bravery is like the other virtues in being the golden mean between opposites.'

'The Golden Mean! That's very good, Larry. I reckon that we're beginning to see what it is to be virtuous. It is to live according to the Golden Mean. And isn't it clear that a person who makes full use of their intelligence to live according to the Golden Mean is almost certain to lead a fulfilling and happy life?'

'You have summed it all up very well, Bob. Yet maybe not all the qualities we admire in a person obey the Golden Mean. Maybe it applies to some virtues but not to others.'

'Can you think of a virtue to which it might not apply?'

'I was thinking about honesty, Bob. It is definitely a virtue in someone to be honest, but it would be silly to say that honesty lies in the middle between being completely truthful and being a total liar.'

'That obviously wouldn't do. Yet maybe that's not the way to think of it.'

'Then how should we think of it?'

'I'm not altogether sure, Larry. Maybe to be honest is neither to exaggerate something nor to downplay it. An honest person is someone who tells it like it is.'

'I don't know what I think about that, Bob. But even if we can account for honesty, there may be other virtues that still don't fit the idea of a Golden Mean.'

'Perhaps so, Larry, but we are not going to discover them today. I've just noticed the time and if I don't get going I will be late for an appointment.'

'In that case, Bob, you had better be off. After all, punctuality is a virtue, and consists in being neither early nor late, but arriving on time. And failing to arrive on time for your appointments makes everyone unhappy.'

The Stoics and Epicureans

ZENO OF CITIUM
c. 334–c. 262 BC

EPICURUS OF SAMOS
c. 341–c. 270 BC

Zeno of Citium was the founder of the Stoic school of philosophy, which met on a *stoa* (or porch) in the agora of ancient Athens. Stoicism continued under the Romans, and included the emperor Marcus Aurelius (121–180 AD) as one of its adherents. The Stoics taught that a wise person does not hanker after what cannot be had and is not affected by misfortune. While others are slaves to their desires, the wise are truly free.

Epicurus of Samos also lived in Athens and was the founder of the philosophy called Epicureanism. Epicureans sought happiness through a quiet, modest and virtuous life, which they taught would bring pleasure and the absence of fear and pain. It is said that Epicurus had a sign above his gate that said, 'Stranger, here you will do well to tarry; here our highest good is pleasure'.

One problem discussed by the Stoics and Epicureans concerns freedom and what is known as determinism. This is the problem addressed by the two cats, Tickle-Tum and Sphinx, in the next story. According to the Stoics, everything that happens has a cause that makes it happen. Yet if everything is made to happen just as it does happen, and couldn't have been otherwise, where is the room for us to decide what to do of our own free will? To this, Zeno is supposed to have said that we are like a dog tied to a cart. We can either go willingly or be forced along. Those who are wise are free because they understand their lot and go along willingly.

The Epicureans also faced this problem because they held that everything is made up of tiny particles of matter mechanically moving through empty space. Since we are composed of such things, how can we be free? Their solution was to say that the atoms must be able to swerve a little from the path they would otherwise take. Given this little bit of free play in the movement of the atoms, our behaviour need not be completely determined.

THE CATS' CONUNDRUM

TICKLE-TUM AND SPHINX SPEND their days sitting together on the high stone wall that separates the park from the gardens of their houses. Occasionally, Tickle-Tum jumps down to look for some morsel in his bowl or to smell the flowers in his garden, and sometimes Sphinx can be found sleeping on the old wicker chair on her porch. Apart from that, they sit on top of the wall and watch the world go by.

That's where they were when an unexpected downpour made them jump down and scurry off to Sphinx's place. Cats hate rain, but there's nothing they can do about it. All that's left is to run for cover.

'That nasty rain,' complained Tickle-Tum, 'it makes me cross. I was just settling in for a nap.'

'There's no point getting your back up, Tickle-Tum. That won't change the weather. Besides, it didn't rain just to spoil your morning.'

'I suppose not,' said Tickle-Tum with a sigh of resignation.

'You know very well that it didn't rain on purpose, you silly cat,' replied Sphinx. 'It rains because things happen up in the clouds that make it rain.'

'I know that,' explained Tickle-Tum. 'I meant that there's really no point in complaining about the weather.'

Sphinx ignored what Tickle-Tum said and carried straight on as if she were delivering a speech. '*Everything* that happens occurs because something makes it happen—whether it's the rain that pours from dark and heavy clouds, or figs that grow in the spring and then again in the summer, or leaves that wither and fall to the ground in their season ...'

'That may be true of nature,' interjected Tickle-Tum, 'but it's not true of us. *We* are not forced to do whatever we do. We decide for ourselves what we will do and what we won't do.'

'As happened when we decided to run for shelter?'

'That's right, Sphinx. The weather may not have had any choice in whether it rained or not, but we decided for ourselves what we would do.'

'You don't think that the rain made us decide to run, Tickle-Tum?'

'I admit that we decided to run because of the rain, Sphinx, but that isn't to say the rain forced the decision upon us.'

'OK, I agree that the rain *alone* didn't make us run for shelter. If we were like ducks, and didn't care about getting wet, we would have stayed put. But cats are not like ducks. We hate getting wet. It's in our nature. So that's also part of the reason why we ran. I would say that it was the rain together with our nature that made us run.'

'But Sphinx, that makes it look as if we didn't decide what to do of our own free will—as if we were made to run just as it was made to rain.'

'That's what puzzles me, Tickle-Tum. What kind of freedom do we have if our decisions and actions come about like all the other events of this world, which simply uncoil like a rope?'

'If you were right, Sphinx, then we would have no kind of freedom at all. But you're not right. I am free to do as I wish. And now that it has stopped raining, I have decided to see whether there is milk in my bowl.'

With that, Tickle-Tum got up and headed off in the direction of his garden, leaving Sphinx to wander back to the wall and ponder a question. Did Tickle-Tum really have the freedom to do as he wished, or was it that he couldn't stop himself checking his bowl all the time because it was in his nature?

While Tickle-Tum was lapping up his milk, he couldn't help thinking about whether Sphinx could be right to say that everything is made to happen exactly as it does happen. If everything were made to happen, then his thoughts and deeds would be made to happen. So he wouldn't really be free to think and do as he wished. Yet it seemed to Tickle-Tum that he was free to think about things, and to wander around his garden or to sit on the wall, just as he pleased. So the world couldn't be as fixed and unbending as Sphinx made out. He kept thinking about this all the while and by the time that he had licked his bowl completely clean he had had an idea.

As Tickle-Tum worked his way back to the wall he could see Sphinx sitting up there majestically, at peace with the world. He wondered what it would be like to be Sphinx and not be ruffled by things.

'I have been chewing over what you said about things being made to happen as they do,' he said, coming up to her. 'Did you mean to say that they are made to happen *exactly* as they do?'

'Absolutely,' replied Sphinx.

'So that every drop of rain that falls is made to fall just when and where it falls?'

'Every drop of rain that falls, and every other thing that happens—right down to the tiniest things that can't even be seen.'

'You don't suppose that there might be room for just a little bit of chance?'

'What do you mean by "a little bit of chance"?' said Sphinx, pricking up her ears.

'Well, couldn't it be that whether a drop of rain falls *exactly* on this spot rather than on that one is due to chance?'

'Do you just mean that the way things happen isn't fully laid down in advance?'

'I mean something like that,' replied Tickle-Tum, who wasn't sure that he really understood what it meant for something to happen by chance.

'Let us suppose for the moment that you are right,' suggested Sphinx. 'What of it?'

'It might be all we need to be able to do things of our own free will,' said Tickle-Tum triumphantly. 'After all, if there's no saying exactly where a raindrop might fall, then there must be freedom enough for us to determine where we jump.'

'So that what we do wouldn't be completely determined by the world about us or by our nature,' offered Sphinx.

'That's it,' replied Tickle-Tum. 'We would be free to do as we wish.'

'But what kind of freedom is that, Tickle-Tum?'

'It is the kind of freedom that makes us responsible for what we do, rather than being like puppets on strings.'

'I see,' said Sphinx doubtfully. 'Didn't you base this on the idea of things happening by chance?'

'I did.'

'So there is always a chance that our decisions might go one way rather than another?'

'That's right.'

'But if our decisions arise by chance, then making a decision is like throwing a dice. We don't decide what number comes up. It turns up by chance and was none of our doing. That's hardly like making up your own mind.'

'So you don't like my idea,' said Tickle-Tum sullenly.

'It doesn't give you what you want,' replied Sphinx coolly. At this unhappy turn of events the two cats sat silently eyeing each other. They felt so irritated that they would have begun hissing at one another if they weren't good-natured.

Presently, a man came into the park with a dog on a lead. The cats watched as the dog strained and pulled in every direction except along the path where the man was headed. Eventually, the man stopped and scolded the dog. Then he forced it to sit and stay still. Every time the dog went to move, the man made it sit back on its haunches. At last, when the dog was obedient, the man tugged on the lead and headed off again, this time with the dog willingly traipsing along behind him.

This distraction was just what the cats needed in order to get over their upset with each other. They continued to watch the dog until it disappeared from view. It was only then that Sphinx began to speak.

'We are like that dog,' she said mysteriously.

'Cats on a lead!' exclaimed Tickle-Tum. 'I've never heard of such a thing.'

'That's not what I mean,' moaned Sphinx. 'The dog couldn't avoid going where it was taken, and it is the same with us.'

'I grant that the dog had no real choice in the matter,' replied Tickle-Tum. 'But we are not made to turn this way and that by being kept on a lead.'

'You're ignoring the invisible lead of nature,' declared Sphinx.

'The invisible lead of nature,' repeated Tickle-Tum, who wasn't sure what to think of that idea.

'We are powerless to break the laws of nature,' Sphinx continued, 'and they determine everything that happens.'

'No matter if we follow along happily or resist every step?' asked Tickle-Tum.

'No matter what,' Sphinx replied. 'And we'll be much happier if we don't spend our lives being frustrated like that dog by trying to do things that we can't do.'

'If you were right,' said Tickle-Tum, 'then there would be no point in trying to do anything.'

'That's not true,' Sphinx corrected. 'There can be every point in setting out to do things you want to do, so long as they are within your powers.'

'I don't follow you,' complained Tickle-Tum. 'A moment ago you said we were like the dog that couldn't do what it wanted. Now you're saying the opposite.'

'Not at all,' Sphinx replied. 'The dog couldn't do what it wanted when it was straining on its lead. But when it trotted along after its master, it went along willingly. So it is with us. Being on nature's lead doesn't mean that you never get to do what you want to do.'

'But the dog had to go wherever it was taken,' said Tickle-Tum. 'So it wasn't really free.'

'It was free when it was doing what it wanted to do,' Sphinx countered with a grin. 'What more is there to freedom than that?'

While Tickle-Tum didn't know how to respond to Sphinx, he had the sneaking suspicion that there was more to freedom than just being able to do what you want to do. It was true that the dog moved along freely when it stopped straining on its lead. Yet that was only because it wanted to do what it had to do. And since Sphinx had insisted that everything is made to happen just as it does, the dog couldn't help wanting what it wanted, in any case. Where's the freedom in that?

Still, Tickle-Tum had to concede that Sphinx was at home in the world. She didn't worry about the weather or constantly check her bowl. She took things as they came. As Tickle-Tum knew only too well, Sphinx was free in a way that he envied.

MEDIEVAL PHILOSOPHY

There now follows a period of over a thousand years, from the decline of the ancient Roman world until the rise of the modern one. Medieval philosophy in Europe was largely a mixture of ancient philosophy and the Christian religion. I am not going to deal with medieval philosophy here. If you are curious about it, you might like to look up Christian scholars such as Saint Augustine (354–430) and Saint Thomas Aquinas (1225–1274).

RENÉ DESCARTES

1596–1650

René Descartes was a French philosopher who also made significant contributions to science and mathematics. He is regarded as the father of modern philosophy and his influence is still felt today. Descartes was a rationalist, which means that he took knowledge to come from reasoning with our minds rather than observing with our senses. This is the opposite of empiricism, which we will meet later in the views of John Locke and David Hume.

I have drawn upon Descartes's *Meditations on First Philosophy* for 'Pipe Dreams'. In his *Meditations*, Descartes sought a firm foundation for knowledge, and he found it in the clear and distinct ideas that came before his mind rather than in the evidence of his senses. He discarded what his senses told him because they had often deceived him in the past, and for all he knew he might have been dreaming. Not only that, it was at least possible that the world he took himself to perceive was an illusion conjured up by an evil demon who was intent upon fooling poor Descartes. Yet, while there may not even have been a physical world, and Descartes may not have had a body with which to perceive things, he did have his thoughts. Descartes's thoughts were one thing that he could not possibly deny. With this observation, he made his famous claim: 'I think, therefore I am'.

Descartes went on to argue that he was essentially a thinking thing or mind altogether distinct from his body. It was with his mind and not his bodily senses that he knew things—even such things as the nature of a lump of wax that was on the table before him. When heated, he knew the wax would soften and melt, appearing altogether different from what it once had been. Yet in his mind he knew it was the very same wax as before. So the wax was a substance known to his mind rather than through the way that it appeared to his senses. Look for all of this as you read 'Pipe Dreams'.

Pipe Dreams

IF YOU WERE TO climb down the drain and crawl along the pipes that run beneath the park, you might come across a frog that lives down there in solitary seclusion. That frog has never ventured far from his underworld and has only a doubtful knowledge of the park or the creatures that inhabit it. While he believes in a world beyond the pipes in which he spends his days, all he really knows of that world are the glimpses that he gets when he jumps out into the drain. The only living things he ever encounters are the creepy-crawlies that inhabit the pipes. But they don't talk as they scurry by, and the frog knows almost nothing about them. For all he can tell, they are mindless mechanisms that have no souls at all. Occasionally, he hears the sound of what seems to be another frog answering his call—although it may just be an echo.

When the frog began to think about it, he realised that there was only one thing he knew for sure. He knew that he was a frog. 'And how do I know that?' said the frog to himself. 'That's easy! I have two powerful legs to hop about, like so. And I can puff up my big soft throat and croak, like this.' The frog began to croak with great satisfaction, until it occurred to him that perhaps he didn't know even this one simple thing—at least, not with *absolute* certainty. For wasn't it just possible that he was only dreaming that he was hopping about and croaking? He had to admit that often enough he had thought that he was doing those things when all the time he was sound asleep and only dreaming that he was hopping and croaking. So perhaps he was dreaming now. As the frog pondered this possibility, an even more unsettling thought popped into his mind. Just suppose that a powerful wizard was tricking him into thinking that he could do these things, when he had never had legs or a throat in the first place. As bizarre as it seemed, in reality he might be a legless and throatless thing—a creature even lowlier than a creepy-crawly—and everything he did could be a dream that was controlled by an evil wizard. Could the frog prove that it wasn't so? No, he could not.

These thoughts so unnerved the frog that he made up his mind to search for something completely solid and certain upon which he could build his knowledge of the world. 'After all,' thought the frog, 'who wants to go through life not really knowing anything?'

While reflecting on this matter, the frog came up with a bright idea. He would set aside all the things that he thought he knew but couldn't actually prove—things that a wizard might well have conjured up—and proceed in this way until he came across something that couldn't conceivably be doubted. Whatever was beyond all possible doubt, you see, was something he could be said to know for sure. From such things he could begin to build an unshakable knowledge of the world. Brilliant!

So it was that the frog began to cast off all those things that he had taken himself to know, as if they were illusions. For how could he know that he heard himself croak if he couldn't be certain that he had a throat with which to croak? How could he know that he felt slime under his legs if he couldn't be certain that he had legs to begin with?

If he couldn't be certain that he had legs and a throat, how could he be sure that he had the rest of his body? Perhaps he was being tricked into thinking that he inhabited the body of a frog when he had no body at all. A wizard could easily perform such a trick. Then he would have no senses with which to perceive anything, and his whole world would be just a fantasy. Even the creepy-crawlies would be unreal—like things in a nightmare that the wizard made up to scare him.

'Wait a minute!' thought the frog. 'It certainly seems to me that I hear myself croak, feel the slime under my legs, and notice creepy-crawlies scurrying by. So even supposing that I have no body, there is no slime, and there are no creepy-crawlies, at least I have these thoughts. And to have these thoughts, I must exist. Of that I can be certain. So even if there is a wicked wizard tricking me at every point, I can be certain that I exist—so long as I am thinking.'

These thoughts so pleased the frog he almost overlooked the fact that, while he could be certain of his own existence, he had no real knowledge of what he was. It is one thing to know that you exist and quite another to know what you are. 'Well, then, what am I?' thought the frog. 'I had previously taken myself to be a frog—a creature that likes to hop and loves to croak. Now that I cannot be certain of any of this, what can I take myself to be?'

To realise that you don't really know what you are is like being swept away by a flood. In his bewilderment, the frog clung to the one thing that kept him afloat—the knowledge of his own existence. It was he who seemed to hear himself croak, who felt as if there were slime under his legs, and who now felt baffled and confused. This very fact suddenly struck the frog as a clue. Not only did he undeniably exist, but it was also beyond doubt that he had these thoughts and feelings. The thoughts and feelings themselves were certainly real even if the things he experienced were not. And they were *his* thoughts and feelings. That couldn't be denied. 'So what am I?' croaked the frog, puffing himself up as far as he could. 'I am a thing that thinks—a thing that has thoughts and feelings and enjoys all kinds of experiences.' With this realisation the frog sat there for ever so long, in astonishment at this discovery. It was as if he had awoken from a deep sleep and knew himself for the first time.

This was only the beginning of the frog's quest for knowledge, which is too long an adventure to recount—except for one other thing that I must tell you.

The frog was so puffed up with his recent discovery that he hardly noticed a balloon that had drifted into the drain. He wouldn't have noticed it at all if the young owner of the balloon hadn't wailed and cried so much. The frog waited until the wailing had died away and then he hopped off along the pipe towards the drain to take a better look.

When he thought it was safe, the frog went out to inspect it. The balloon was large and round and shiny. It was stretched tight, and it squeaked and bounced when he touched it. The frog was delighted. So he prodded it once more. It bounced again. Only this time the balloon hit the rim of an old tin can that was lying in the drain, whereupon it suddenly began shrieking and rushing about. The frog leapt back into the pipe, only to be followed by the screaming monster. When it came to rest and the frog was certain that it was dead, he went over to inspect it once again. Only it wasn't large and round and shiny anymore, but small and flat and dull. When, gingerly, he touched it, it was limp instead of taut, and it didn't squeak or bounce. It lay there like a shrivelled finger.

The frog thought about the balloon. Once it was big and round. Now it was small and flat. It had been shiny. Now it was dull. At first it squeaked and bounced when he touched it, but now it was silent and still. So what he knew as the balloon could not be merely what he saw and felt and heard. For it was the same balloon, whether it was round or flat, shiny or dull, taut or limp, squeaky or silent, bouncy or still. And being the same thing all along, the balloon must be something besides these changing attributes.

Yet what was it that continued to exist through all these changes? Surely it was only something that occupied space, and was moveable and stretchy. For the balloon continued to take up some space, whether large or small; it moved from one place to another and could be stretched to one extent or another. The balloon was therefore that stretchy, moveable thing that continued to exist throughout all the changes.

The frog puffed himself up and was about to give in to the pleasure of a loud and long spell of croaking, when he suddenly became deflated. He realised that there was a further problem.

If the changing appearance of the balloon was known to his senses, with what did he know it as it really was?

It was then that the frog had a brainwave. It struck him that his knowledge of the balloon was like his knowledge of himself. Earlier he had discovered that he clearly and certainly knew himself through the thoughts in his own mind and not through his senses. Now it occurred to him that he also knew of the balloon with his mind rather than his senses. For only his mind was capable of judging that something remained the same throughout all the changes and of understanding what it was.

So the frog came to attribute all real knowledge of himself and his world to the powers of his mind—and not to his senses. You might think that only a creature condemned to live in so dark and murky a world as the frog's could believe such a thing. Nothing could have been further from the minds of the creatures that lived above ground as they basked in the bright afternoon sunshine.

THE BRITISH EMPIRICISTS

JOHN LOCKE
1632–1704

GEORGE BERKELEY
1685–1753

DAVID HUME
1711–1776

John Locke, George Berkeley and David Hume are known as British empiricists. They are called British because Locke was English, Berkeley was Irish and Hume was Scottish. Empiricism is the view that our knowledge comes from experience that we gain through our senses. It is opposed to the idea that reason is the basis of our knowledge.

The next story, 'Scottie and John Bull', is based on the philosophy of Hume and Locke. I have not gone into Berkeley's philosophy because he is most famous for claiming that to exist is to be perceived. That is to say, everything exists just as a perception—something in front of the mind. This curious view would need a separate story all to itself.

John Locke claimed that when we are born our minds are like a blank slate upon which experience begins to write. There is no such thing as an innate idea. So a newborn baby has no idea of anything at all before it encounters the world through its senses and then experiences what happens in its mind. Locke took all of our ideas, whether simple or complex, to arise in this way.

Similarly, David Hume maintained that all of our ideas arise from impressions that we gain through our senses, and from this he went on to draw some very sceptical conclusions. He claimed that sometimes we have no real idea of what we are talking about because there are no impressions from which the idea could arise. The waterwheel in 'Scottie and John Bull' provides an illustration of this concept. There we encounter Hume's claim that we are never aware of any force in nature by which one thing brings about another. We think that we perceive such forces, but it is an illusion produced by the way our minds work. We are so used to seeing one thing, which we call the cause, followed by another, which we call its effect, that the two become associated in our minds. So when the cause occurs, we immediately anticipate its effect, and we mistake this movement from cause to effect in our own minds for an awareness of the power by which the one brings about the other.

SCOTTIE AND JOHN BULL

THE AFTERNOON IS HOT and all the benches in the park are empty, except for the one shaded by the giant fig tree. On it sits a woman with her head buried in a book, while her two dogs amuse themselves playing with a bright red ball. One dog is a terrier called Scottie. The other is a bulldog whose name is John Bull—although everyone calls him JB.

The dogs are playing a game that goes like this: one of the dogs holds the ball between his teeth, twists his head and shoulders back and forth, and throws the ball with all his might. The other dog runs after it. Because they can't throw the ball very far, they make the game more interesting by having the thrower chase after the other dog and try to wrestle the ball from him.

Meanwhile, the woman has put down her book and wandered over to talk to a man who is cuddling a newborn pup. The puppy is so young that when the man bends over to gently place it on the path it trembles, and the owner has to steady it for a moment to help it stand.

The puppy has caught the attention of Scottie and JB, who trot over to meet it. While JB looks on in amusement, Scottie picks up the ball, twists back and forth and throws it for the puppy to chase.

The puppy does not move.

Scottie looks at the puppy and then turns towards the ball.

Still the puppy doesn't move. So Scottie fetches the ball himself and begins the whole thing over again—with exactly the same result.

Scottie once again retrieves the ball, drops it right in front of the puppy and watches him closely. But all the puppy does is stare at the ball, as if trying to see what is there.

Since there is no point in trying to play with the puppy, the two dogs amble off.

'He doesn't know how to play ball, JB. He has no idea.'

'I doubt he even knows what a ball is, Scottie. He's probably never seen one before.'

'He has seen one now.'

'But could he see it *as a ball*, Scottie? Maybe all he could see was a round red patch.'

'Do you mean to tell me that he can't tell the difference between a ball and a spot of colour?'

'That may be so, Scottie. He wasn't born knowing about balls, and without more experience how could he know what he is looking at?'

'I guess you're right, JB. It certainly looked as if he couldn't make much out of the ball. But if he doesn't know a ball when he sees one, then he also won't be able to make much out of other things—like bones, trees, lampposts, fences and cats.'

'Yes, Scottie, I suppose that he has very little idea of anything yet and that experience must teach him.'

'If that's so, JB, then the same must have been true of us. When we were born, we would have had no idea about anything either.'

'That's right, Scottie. It must have been only as we gained experience of things that our ideas of them started to form.'

'Do you know what, JB? Until now I had never thought about where ideas come from. Yet, thinking about that puppy, isn't it clear that all of our ideas come from experience?'

'I think so, Scottie. And it implies that we are born entirely without them.'

Scottie and JB were sniffing along the garden fences that bordered one side of the park when something caught their attention.

'Do you hear that trickling sound, Scottie?'

'I do. It seems to be coming from the other side of the fence somewhere down there. Let's go and find out.'

The two dogs worked their way along the fence, peering through the cracks between the palings, and soon they came across the strange contraption that was making the noise. Water was flowing from a bamboo spout so that it filled little bamboo cups mounted on a wheel that stood in a pond. When a cup filled with water from the spout, the wheel turned and the cup went down, only to be replaced by the next cup, which also filled with water and then moved down. And so on it went, cup after cup. As the cups came down and around, they poured their water into the pond and then came up the other side, upside down. After they had come full circle they were upright again, and ready to be filled by water from the spout.

The dogs watched in fascination as the waterwheel with its little cups turned around and around.

'That's new, JB.'

'Yes. What do you suppose it's for?'

'I don't know. Maybe it's to scare away cats.'

'How does it work?'

'I'll bet that it doesn't work, JB. If you want to scare off cats, then you should get a dog.'

'No, Scottie, I mean how does the whole thing keep turning around?'

'I see what you're after. It must be the water in the cups. Whenever a cup fills with water it goes down and the wheel turns, while the cups without any water in them come up the other side. You can see that happening again and again, cup after cup.'

JB sat back on his haunches. 'I've got the idea of it now, Scottie—filling a cup with water *forces* it to go down.'

'Where did you get that idea, JB? You can't see the force you're talking about.'

'But the idea of it is very clear in my mind.'

'Are you sure, JB? Didn't we agree earlier that we have no ideas except those that we gain from experience? So if you can't see the force you're talking about, how could you have come by such an idea?'

'I don't know. It must have come from somewhere.'

'But from where? You said yourself that we aren't born knowing such things. Just think about that puppy. It could have no idea of such a force. It wouldn't know what you're talking about.'

JB got up off his haunches, peered through the palings, and fixed his gaze on the waterwheel.

'You can look as much as you like, JB. All you'll experience is a cup being filled with water and then the cup going down—the same thing, again and again—without ever seeing the force you're looking for.'

'Then there is no way to explain the feeling that there is such a force, and we really are in the poo.'

'Don't whine, JB. I have a solution.'

'Do you, Scottie? What is it?'

'I suppose it's like this. When you constantly see the cups filling with water and then going down, you can hardly think of a cup filling without also thinking of its going down. The two things become so connected in your mind that the thought of one summons up the thought of the other.'

'That sounds right, Scottie, but I don't see how it helps.'

'I haven't finished, JB. I'll tell you how that solves your problem if you'll only listen.'

'I'm listening, Scottie. Go on.'

'When you look at a cup filling with water, your mind runs ahead and thinks of it falling.'

'And that's because you've seen it happen so many times, Scottie.'

'That's right. Now here's the point. When you look at the cup filling with water and expect it to fall, you mistake this expectation for being aware of some force that makes it fall.'

'Do you mean to say that our own expectations fool us into thinking that we're aware of some force?'

'Yes, I do.'

'I don't know what to say, Scottie. I suppose it could be right.'

'I'm surprised at you, JB. I thought it was brilliant.'

'I don't deny its brilliance, Scottie, but that doesn't make it right. Besides, there may be other difficulties with this view of ours that we have no real ideas of anything except those that come to us through our experience.'

'Even if you are right about that, JB, we have done quite enough thinking for now. Thinking makes me hungry. I know it's not nearly dinnertime yet, but how about going over and showing how hungry we are, so that she will take us home.'

'How about this, Scottie?' JB adopted a hangdog look and let out a pathetic noise.

'That's very well done, JB. Let's try it on her.'

And so the two dogs trotted off across the park towards the woman with the book, intent on an early dinner.

IMMANUEL KANT

1724–1804

Immanuel Kant was a German philosopher who lived all his life in the Prussian town of Königsberg. He tried to resolve the dispute between the rationalists and the empiricists by discovering the conditions underlying all human knowledge. Instead of asking how we come to know about the world—whether it is through our senses or by the powers of reason—he wanted to discover what makes it possible for us to come by any knowledge at all. His answer was that we cannot know about the world independently of our senses, but that all of our experience is shaped by forms of understanding that are built into our minds from the outset. This is a bit like saying that a computer doesn't come to store any information unless we feed that information into it, but that it can't process the information unless it already possesses programs that can make sense of it.

Kant is also famous for his contribution to ethics. He tried to show that you can always tell whether what you propose to do is morally acceptable by asking what would happen if we made it a rule for everyone to behave in that way. If you cannot consistently will everyone to behave that way, then what you're proposing to do isn't morally acceptable. For example, suppose that you promised to do something but you never intended to do it. Kant asks what would happen if we made it a rule for everyone to do the same. In that case, we couldn't trust anyone to do what they promised to do. And that is as good as to say that there would no longer be such a thing as a genuine promise. Kant thought that this showed what you were proposing to do wasn't morally acceptable.

In 'Immanuel's Idea', a boy makes this discovery by reflecting on his failure to keep his own promise and goes on to think about whether the same applies to other things you ought not to do.

Immanuel's Idea

On her deck overlooking the park, Mrs Allworthy and Immanuel are enjoying afternoon tea and cakes. Mrs Allworthy looks after Immanuel after school until his mother comes home from work. There's nothing Immanuel likes better than to talk to Mrs Allworthy. For some reason he finds it much more interesting to talk to her than to do his homework. It should be said that he's also very fond of Mrs Allworthy's little cakes. So much so, that the very thought of Mrs Allworthy conjures up the smell of them cooking and the taste of the icing that she puts on top.

In between mouthfuls of cake, Immanuel was discussing his dog, Trixie. He got her for his birthday, but only after pestering his mother for months about getting a dog and promising again and again that he would feed the dog and take it for a walk every day. The trouble was, Immanuel so desperately wanted a dog that he promised these things even though he knew in his heart that he couldn't be relied upon to do them.

'I am surprised at you promising to do something you knew you wouldn't do, Immanuel.'

'My mother kept telling me that she had enough to do without looking after a dog, Mrs Allworthy. It was the only way I could get her to give in.'

'That doesn't sound like you, Immanuel.'

'I know. What I did was wrong.'

'Now your poor mother has to look after Trixie as well as you, all because you made a false promise.'

'Even if I had been honest, I would have still broken my promise.'

'So it's wrong to make honest promises that you don't keep, just as it's wrong to make false promises in the first place.'

'Yes.'

'Why is that?'

'What do you mean, Mrs Allworthy? Everyone knows that it's wrong to do such things.'

'If everyone knows that it's wrong, Immanuel, then you ought to be able to tell me why it's wrong. I'll leave you to think about it while I go and put more tea in the pot. You may as well have the last little cake while you're at it.'

'Would you like another cup of milky tea, dear?'

'Yes, please, Mrs Allworthy.'

'There are no more cakes, I'm afraid.'

'That's OK.'

'Now, where were we?'

'We were talking about what's wrong with people breaking their promises.'

'Oh, yes. What if everyone went around breaking their promises? What could be wrong with that?'

'Don't be silly, Mrs Allworthy. If people behaved like that, then you couldn't trust anyone to keep their promises. You would never know if they meant what they said.'

'And would it be wrong just because we couldn't trust people to keep their promises?'

'It's not just that, Mrs Allworthy. People might say they promise to do something, but they might as well have said that they don't really intend to do it, or that they'll wait and see. That's not promising.'

'No, Immanuel, it's not.'

'If no one could be trusted to keep their promises, then there would be no such thing as promising.'

'That's very interesting, Immanuel. I wonder whether what you say applies to other things besides promising.'

'What do you mean, Mrs Allworthy?'

'Well, dear, we showed that it can't be right to break your promises by asking what would happen if we made it a rule for everyone to behave like that. Suppose we were to ask whether we would want everyone to do other things that someone might be tempted to do.'

'What kinds of things, Mrs Allworthy?'

'Well, not giving back something that was loaned to you, for instance.'

'Like the time I loaned that game to David and he tried to keep it?'

'Yes, that's the kind of thing I mean.'

'If everyone were to behave like David, then no one would loan anything to anyone.'

'In that case, there would be no such thing as loaning.'

'Hey, that's what happened with promising. There couldn't be such a thing as promising if no one could be trusted to keep their word, and loaning things couldn't be made to work if you could never rely upon people to give back what they were loaned.'

'That's true, Immanuel.'

'I get it, Mrs Allworthy. If we want to know whether it is alright to do something we are tempted to do, then we only need to ask whether we would want everybody to behave like that.'

'That's right, Immanuel. And if it turns out like it did with promising and loaning, we would immediately know that it's wrong. We don't have to ask whether we will get away with it this time or not. We know that it's wrong in principle.'

'That's amazing, Mrs Allworthy. Can we try the idea on something else?'

'Of course we can, Immanuel. But it will have to wait for another day, because I can hear your mother at the gate.'

THE UTILITARIANS

JEREMY BENTHAM
1748–1832

JOHN STUART MILL
1806–1873

Jeremy Bentham was a philosopher and social reformer who, together with John Stuart Mill's father, James Mill, argued for what is called utilitarianism. This is the view that an action is morally good if it produces the greatest overall happiness of people. By the 'greatest happiness', Bentham meant the most pleasure and the least pain for all concerned.

Once you begin to think about it, you can see that their view differs greatly from Kant's. He argued that there is a strict moral law which tells us that it is our moral duty never to do things such as lie and steal, no matter what the consequences. Bentham, on the other hand, said that we should always consider the consequences of our actions in deciding what it is right to do—not just as they affect us, of course, but others as well.

John Stuart Mill continued arguing for utilitarianism, but insisted on the distinction between higher and lower pleasures, claiming that intellectual and spiritual pleasures are superior to physical ones, so that 'it is better to be a human dissatisfied than a pig satisfied; better to be Socrates dissatisfied than a fool satisfied'. Look out for this claim in 'Rats Should Be Happy Too'. Rats, of course, tell the story and Mill was talking about the happiness of people. Still, Bentham had already recognised that utilitarianism could be extended to other creatures—a view taken up more recently by some utilitarians.

Rats Should Be Happy Too

ALONG THE DRAIN, AT the back of the park, creepers and vines have overgrown the bushes, creating a thicket. Its dense and tangled undergrowth protects the burrows of creatures who live near the water such as Whiskers and Nip. Like all their friends and relations—of whom there are many—the rats never venture out except when they think it is safe. For rats are regarded as the lowest of creatures, and a dog or a cat will just as surely pick on a rat as a spider will pounce on a fly.

'Did you ever see a rat being given a fair go?' asked Whiskers. 'Everyone thinks that you can do what you like to rats, as if we had no feelings.'

'That's true,' replied Nip. 'We rats have as much right as anyone else to be happy and yet we constantly live in fear for our lives.'

The two rats twitched and scanned the grass as they spoke.

'In a better world,' Nip continued, 'it would make no difference whether you were a dog or a cat or a rat.'

'So that *anyone's* happiness would be just as important as everyone else's,' concluded Whiskers. Then she added, 'And it should also matter *how* happy we are—not just that we are more happy than sad.'

'That's true,' Nip agreed.

'So that we should try to make the world as happy a place as we can,' suggested Whiskers.

'Yes,' said Nip. 'That's the right thing to do.'

With these thoughts of a better world for the likes of Whiskers and Nip, the two rats went back to nibbling the seeds of the plants that grew in a thick and tangled web all around them.

While Whiskers was cleaning herself she watched in amusement as Nip tried to deal with a flea that was on his tail. In trying to get at the flea, Nip was turning around and around in circles.

'Hey, Nip,' said Whiskers, 'before you end up biting off your tail, how about giving some thought to the happiness of fleas.'

'Very funny!' exclaimed Nip, finally managing to dislodge the flea.

'I'm serious,' replied Whiskers, who loved to tease Nip. 'If other creatures should show some thought for the happiness of rats, why shouldn't you take account of the happiness of that flea?'

'Don't be silly,' said Nip. 'There's no such thing as the happiness of fleas.'

'Fleas take pleasure in biting,' Whiskers suggested, 'and what is happiness but taking pleasure in things?'

'Fleas might have their own little pleasures,' Nip responded, 'but they are hardly worth worrying about.'

Whiskers scratched her head and thought for a minute. 'So you're saying that the pain you experience when a flea bites you far outweighs any pleasure the flea might get,' she said at last.

'And therefore that the flea shouldn't bite me,' Nip concluded.

'You try telling that to the flea!' exclaimed Whiskers.

'Anyway,' said Nip, 'a flea's happiness in biting someone would have to be the lowest form of pleasure imaginable.'

'Oh, so there are lower and higher forms of pleasure,' Whiskers concluded.

'Definitely,' replied Nip. 'You can't tell me that the lowly form of pleasure that might be possible for a flea is anything like the higher kind of pleasure that a creature like a rat can enjoy.'

'If that's so, then maybe a rat isn't capable of the even higher kind of pleasure that cats and dogs can have,' teased Whiskers.

'That's going too far,' muttered Nip. 'Though I admit that some noble creatures are capable of higher pleasures than the rest of us—creatures like that bird Snub Nose, for instance.'

'Do you mean the philosopher who devotes his life to questioning everyone?'

Nip nodded.

'But he's never happy with the answers that anyone gives,' said Whiskers.

'It would be better to be Snub Nose dissatisfied, than a flea satisfied,' replied Nip.

Whiskers had to admit that Nip was right about the flea and the philosopher. Though she had a suspicion that once you admitted the difference between them it wouldn't be long before the happiness of some animals was judged to be far more important than the happiness of others. Then they would be right back where they had started, with the happiness of rats being a matter of very little consequence.

Nip ran along the open drain and scurried up an old apple tree. Then he climbed out to the end of a branch that was hanging over the water and began to gnaw on an apple. The branch was so thin that each time Nip strained forward to take a bite, it sprang up and down, ever more vigorously. Then the inevitable happened. Whiskers watched as the branch went wild and Nip was flung into the drain. That would have been the end of him if rats weren't good swimmers, but it was only a moment before Nip reappeared, heading for dry land.

'Just look at you,' said Whiskers, as a bedraggled Nip staggered towards her, 'and all for a few bites at an apple.'

'It didn't really hurt,' replied Nip, shaking all over.

'Don't tell me that it was worth it,' Whiskers countered. 'Whatever pleasure you got from going after that apple hardly makes up for what happened to you.'

'Allright!' replied Nip. 'It was a silly thing to do. But nothing would have made me happier than to have eaten that apple right down to the core.'

'I understand that,' said Whiskers consolingly, 'but you're not going to end up happy unless you're sensible. And if you act foolishly, then you are going to make those around you unhappy too.'

'What business is it of others if I take risks?' Nip snorted.

'If you had drowned, then I would have been very unhappy,' said Whiskers, 'and so would all your friends and relations.'

Nip was comforted by the thought that Whiskers was right. He had to concede that he needed to take other rats' happiness into account when he was thinking about what he wanted to do. That reminded him of something. 'It's like the rule that we came up with earlier,' he said.

'What rule?' inquired Whiskers.

'The rule which says that the right thing to do is whatever would lead to the greatest overall happiness.'

Whiskers scratched her head, as she was in the habit of doing when she was thinking. Then she said, 'That was about right and wrong, and this is about being sensible rather than silly.'

'The same applies to both,' replied Nip.

'How do you mean?' said Whiskers.

'I mean that we should judge *everything* that we do by how it affects our happiness,' Nip explained.

'I see,' said Whiskers. 'And by "our happiness" you mean to include the happiness of all those around us?'

'I mean the happiness of all creatures,' remarked Nip.

This utterance must have impressed Whiskers as much as it surprised Nip himself, because the two rats fell silent. Each was left to ponder what it meant. That they should take account of the happiness of all creatures in what they did meant not only that the happiness of a rat counted for something, but that everyone should consider the welfare of all creatures who have any feelings at all.

Ludwig Wittgenstein

1889–1951

Ludwig Wittgenstein was one of the most influential philosophers of the twentieth century. His philosophical brilliance was recognised when he was a student at Cambridge University in England, and he produced some very significant early work. Then he moved away from philosophy, worked as a primary school teacher in his native Austria, designed a house for his sister and did other odd jobs. Eventually, he was persuaded to return to

Cambridge, where he rejected his earlier philosophical work and created a very different philosophy that continued to occupy him throughout the later part of his life.

'Tree Talk' is based on the later philosophy of Wittgenstein. It introduces us to his idea that philosophical problems are really puzzles that arise because we don't understand how language works, and that by looking carefully at the way we use language, we can make our philosophical worries go away. In 'Tree Talk', this idea is applied to the philosophy of Socrates and it is suggested that it can also be used to criticise the work of other philosophers. Along the way, we will also encounter Wittgenstein's famous concept of language games, which is meant to help us to see how we use words quite differently for different purposes, so that there is no such thing as *the* meaning of a word.

Wittgenstein is not alone in criticising the work of earlier philosophers. That's common in philosophy. Every age and society needs to work on philosophy for itself. If we become philosophically lazy and self-satisfied, we will end up with nothing but worn-out, hand-me-down ideas.

Tree Talk

'**I HAVE STOOD HERE** patiently listening to all those creatures chatter, squawk, bark, talk, meow, croak and squeak—particularly that old bird Snub Nose, who thinks that he can park himself on me all day and talk nonsense. He thinks that what he says is deep, but it is only because he is like a child who doesn't know how to use language properly. If you think that you have glimpsed some profound truth in their mutterings, then I would say that you too have been bewitched by language. It is high time for me to cast off that spell. So try to sit still for once and listen carefully to the rustle of my leaves.

'I'll begin by telling you a story. Yesterday I overheard a little girl called Jessica complaining to her mother about a bruise on her leg. Her mother tried to comfort her by saying that in a day or two the bruise would go away. When Jessica asked where it would go, her mother laughed and said that it wouldn't go anywhere. This made Jessica very confused and it had to be explained to her that saying her bruise would go away was not to say that it would go somewhere else, like when Jessica and her family went away on holiday. You see, Jessica thought that the words "go away" always meant the same thing. But of course bruises don't go away in the same kind of way that people go away on holiday.

'I am telling you this story because I think that it isn't only three-year-olds like Jessica who don't know their way around with language. Take Snub Nose. He thinks that we must always mean exactly the same thing whenever we use the word "good", so that every good thing must have something in common that makes it good—and he has spent the best part of his life trying to find out what that is! Isn't he just like a three-year-old? Why couldn't to "be good" be like to "go away", so that its meaning changes when we use it on one occasion or another?

'Are you paying attention? You're so fidgety, you young people. If I were to say that you should learn to be patient with an old tree, who will finish what he has to say all in *good time*, surely that has nothing in common with talking about someone doing a *good deed*. To finish something all in good time is to do it without rushing, whereas to perform a good deed is to do something virtuous. To say that they must have something in common that makes them both good is about as silly as saying that there must be something in common between your homework being as *good* as done and giving the other team a *good* beating.

'Don't think that I have the time to tell you how to undo all the knots in which these creatures have tied themselves. I have better things to do. But I'll give you a clue. You must have noticed how they keep harping on about there being one thing lying at the end of their quests. How everything in the universe must have come from the one thing. How our knowledge must come from the one source, whether it is the mind or the senses. How there must be one ultimate rule that can tell us how to be happy, or to be good. Even how all the scruffy dogs of this world are not real, but in the end only the one ideal dog is really real. What nonsense! Just because ordinary dogs don't quite measure up, they say that there must be something else that fully answers to "dog"—the ideal dog. I say again, these philosophers are like little children who haven't yet learned their way around in language. If they had been around as long as an old gnarled tree like me, things might be different.

'I'll tell you one more thing, so pay attention! I am sure that you know all kinds of games. I know of some too. Even though it's getting dark now, from up here I can see way beyond the park to the field where people play football, and if I look down I can just make out a skipping game chalked on the path. Today, Scottie and JB played that silly game they made up, and yesterday Bob and Larry were playing chess on the bench next to my trunk. I have heard of card games and board games, of computer games and court games, and of games like guessing games that can be played just about anywhere with nothing at all. Here is a question for you. What do all these games have in common that makes them games—which things that are not games lack? So far as I can see, there isn't anything at all.

'Games are like members of a family. While they resemble each other in all kinds of ways, there is no one thing that makes them all games. In one game, you kick a ball through a goal, in another you try to direct it where your opponent can't return it and in yet another you aim to knock your opponent's ball out of the ring. In this game you take your turn by throwing a die, in that one you do so by taking a card from the deck and in yet another you do it by spinning a wheel. Not all games have balls, or goals or rings, of course, and you don't always take turns in games.

'Why am I telling you all this? It is because we play games with language too. We tell jokes, sing songs, barrack for our team and make up riddles. We keep lists, write reminders, make promises and send greetings. There is no end to the language games we can play. And just as what it means to throw a ball changes from one ball game to another, so what a word means changes when we use it in one language game or another. And when we use words differently they have different meanings.

'These creatures you have been listening to think that the same words always have the same meaning. As I said, they are like little children who simply don't know how language is used. If only they were to look and see how we actually use language, they wouldn't be so puzzled.

'I don't know whether you have followed all that. But I'll tell you what. You shouldn't be mucking about out here in the park at this time of night. If I were your parent, I wouldn't allow it. You had better be off home before the bats come and get you. Go on, then. Off with you!'

Teaching Ethics in Schools

A new approach to moral education

Philip Cam

Teaching Ethics in Schools provides a fresh approach to moral education, and presents ethical thinking and reasoning as a dynamic and essential aspect of school life.

Part One provides a clear introduction to the theoretical premise of reflection and collaborative inquiry. It draws on the history of philosophy in succinct terms, and relates this to contemporary school contexts, to support teachers in their conceptual understanding.

Part Two provides an array of activities, exercises and discussion points as stimuli for teachers to adapt and apply across diverse subject areas, throughout all stages of schooling. The focus lies in preparing students to think reflectively, to question and probe, and ultimately to develop their own enhanced capacity for ethical reasoning, good moral judgment and considerate conduct, both within the classroom and beyond.

Teaching Ethics in Schools effectively guides teachers in addressing the core tenets of Ethical Understanding, a 'general capability' within the Australian Curriculum.

sales@acer.edu.au | 03 9277 5447 | Order online: http://acer.ac/pcam
www.acer.edu.au/publications/education

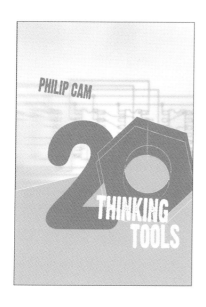

Twenty Thinking Tools

Philip Cam

Twenty Thinking Tools supports the development of collaborative inquiry-based teaching and learning through class discussion and small-group work throughout school and across all educational contexts. It introduces teachers to the theory and practice of collaborative inquiry, and provides an easy-to-follow guide to the tools that students will acquire as they learn to examine issues and explore ideas.

Beginning with an Introductory Toolkit, *Twenty Thinking Tools* shows teachers how to strengthen students' abilities to ask insightful questions, to look at problems and issues from various points of view, to explore disagreements reasonably, to make appropriate use of examples, to draw needful distinctions, and generally to develop their imaginative, conceptual and logical abilities in order to gain a deeper knowledge and understanding of all kinds of subject matter.

The Intermediate and Advanced Toolkits show teachers how to encourage students to make appropriate use of such things as counterexamples, criteria, generalisation, informal reasoning and elementary deductive logic. The Toolkits also include devices for distinguishing between different kinds of questions, for tracking disagreement and for recording discussion.

Containing examples, activities and exercises, *Twenty Thinking Tools* is indispensable for teachers wanting to assist students in investigating the nature of ethical concepts and in understanding how reasoning can assist with ethical judgment, in line with Australian Curriculum requirements.

sales@acer.edu.au | 03 9277 5447 | Order online: http://acer.ac/pcam
www.acer.edu.au/publications/education